How To Start A Business In Canada

Ali Rastegari

Chapters

Chapter 1: Introduction to Canadian Entrepreneurship
- Understanding the Canadian business landscape
- Benefits and challenges of starting a business in Canada
- Key industries and opportunities

Chapter 2: Market Research and Idea Validation
- Conducting market research to identify business opportunities
- Evaluating the feasibility of your business idea
- Understanding customer needs and preferences

Chapter 3: Legal and Regulatory Considerations
- Business structures in Canada: Sole proprietorship, partnership, corporation, etc.
- Registering your business and obtaining necessary licenses and permits
- Understanding tax obligations and compliance

Chapter 4: Crafting a Solid Business Plan
- Elements of a successful business plan
- Creating a vision, mission, and business goals
- Financial projections and budgeting

Chapter 5: Financing Your Business
- Exploring funding options: Loans, grants, venture capital, and angel investors
- Preparing a compelling pitch for investors
- Managing personal finances during the early stages

Chapter 6: Building a Strong Team
- Identifying key roles and hiring the right talent
- Creating a positive company culture and promoting diversity
- Employee rights and labor laws in Canada

Chapter 7: Setting Up Your Business Location
- Choosing the right location for your business
- Leasing agreements and commercial property considerations

- Remote work and virtual office options

Chapter 8: Developing a Marketing Strategy
- Understanding your target market and customer segmentation
- Online and offline marketing channels in Canada
- Building brand awareness and customer acquisition techniques

Chapter 9: Creating a Strong Online Presence
- Building and optimizing a business website
- Leveraging social media and content marketing
- Utilizing e-commerce platforms and digital marketing tools

Chapter 10: Managing Finances and Accounting
- Setting up a bookkeeping and accounting system
- Tracking expenses, revenue, and financial reports
- Understanding Canadian financial regulations

Chapter 11: Navigating Government Support and Incentive Programs
- Identifying government programs for startups and small businesses
- Grants, subsidies, and tax incentives available in Canada
- Engaging with business development organizations

Chapter 12: Protecting Your Intellectual Property
- Understanding intellectual property rights in Canada
- Trademarks, patents, and copyrights registration
- Enforcing and defending your intellectual property

Chapter 13: Managing Risk and Insurance
- Types of business insurance required in Canada
- Risk assessment and mitigation strategies
- Protecting against liability and unexpected events

Chapter 14: Scaling Your Business
- Strategies for growth and expansion
- Exploring international markets and exporting opportunities
- Building partnerships and alliances

Chapter 15: Adapting to Technological Advancements
- Embracing digital transformation for competitive advantage
- Cloud computing, artificial intelligence, and automation in business
- Cybersecurity and data protection measures

Chapter 16: Building Customer Loyalty and Relations
- Customer service best practices
- Creating loyalty programs and incentives
- Managing feedback and handling customer complaints

Chapter 17: Sustainability and Corporate Social Responsibility
- Implementing environmentally friendly practices
- Social initiatives and community engagement
- The importance of ethical business conduct

Chapter 18: Balancing Work-Life and Wellbeing
- Overcoming entrepreneurial burnout
- Stress management and work-life balance
- Promoting wellness in the workplace

Chapter 19: Exit Strategies and Succession Planning
- Preparing for business succession or sale
- Valuing your business and negotiation tactics
- Ensuring a smooth transition for your business

Chapter 20: The Future of Canadian Entrepreneurship
- Emerging trends and opportunities in the Canadian market
- Innovations and technologies to watch out for
- Inspiring stories of successful Canadian entrepreneurs

Epilogue: Your Journey as a Canadian Entrepreneur
- Reflecting on your progress and achievements
- Continuous learning and growth in the business world
- Contributing to the Canadian economy and society as an entrepreneur.

Chapter 1: Introduction to Canadian Entrepreneurship

Canada, known for its diverse landscapes, rich culture, and friendly people, also offers a vibrant business environment that fosters entrepreneurship and innovation. In this chapter, we will delve into the world of Canadian entrepreneurship, understanding the business landscape, exploring the benefits and challenges of starting a business in the country, and identifying key industries and opportunities that await aspiring entrepreneurs.

1.1 Understanding the Canadian Business Landscape

Canada boasts a strong and stable economy, making it an attractive destination for both domestic and international entrepreneurs. The country's economy is characterized by its natural resources, manufacturing, technology, and service sectors, among others. Some key aspects of the Canadian business landscape include:

- Economic Stability: Canada is renowned for its stable economy, which has weathered global financial crises relatively well. The country's fiscal policies, sound banking system, and prudent regulations contribute to its economic resilience.

- Supportive Business Environment: The Canadian government actively encourages entrepreneurship and offers various programs, grants, and incentives to support startups and small businesses. Additionally, a robust legal framework and protection of property rights create a secure environment for investors and entrepreneurs.

- Global Trade Opportunities: Canada is an open economy with strong ties to international markets. Entrepreneurs can leverage trade agreements and expand their businesses globally, benefiting from access to markets around the world.

- Multicultural Market: Canada's diverse population presents an excellent opportunity for businesses to cater to a broad range of tastes and preferences. Understanding and embracing cultural diversity can be a key factor in the success of a business in the Canadian market.

1.2 Benefits of Starting a Business in Canada

As an aspiring entrepreneur, launching a business in Canada offers numerous advantages:

- Strong Infrastructure: Canada boasts excellent infrastructure, including reliable transportation, communication networks, and modern facilities that support businesses in their day-to-day operations.

- Highly Educated Workforce: The country is home to a well-educated and skilled workforce, which can contribute to the success and growth of businesses across various sectors.

- Quality of Life: Canada consistently ranks high in terms of quality of life, making it an attractive destination for entrepreneurs looking to live and work in a safe, stable, and prosperous environment.

- Access to Funding: Entrepreneurs in Canada have access to various funding options, including government grants, venture capital firms, angel investors, and traditional banking institutions.

- Innovation and Research: The country places a strong emphasis on research and development, with government support for innovation in key industries, making it an ideal location for tech startups and businesses focused on cutting-edge advancements.

1.3 Challenges of Starting a Business in Canada

While Canada offers a favorable environment for entrepreneurship, aspiring business owners should be aware of the challenges they might encounter:

- Regulatory Compliance: Navigating through the complexities of business regulations and compliance requirements can be daunting for newcomers. Understanding and adhering to federal, provincial, and municipal regulations is crucial to avoid legal issues.

- Market Competition: The Canadian market can be highly competitive, especially in densely populated urban centers. Entrepreneurs need to develop unique value propositions and differentiation strategies to stand out from competitors.

- Seasonal Industries: Certain regions in Canada experience extreme weather conditions, leading to seasonal industries. Entrepreneurs in such sectors need to plan and manage their businesses accordingly to survive off-peak periods.

- Access to Talent: While Canada has a skilled workforce, certain industries face talent shortages. Hiring the right employees with the necessary skills and experience can be challenging in some regions.

1.4 Key Industries and Opportunities

Canada's diverse economy presents a wide array of opportunities for aspiring entrepreneurs. Some key industries and sectors with significant growth potential include:

- Technology and Innovation: Canada has a thriving tech ecosystem, with hubs in cities like Toronto, Vancouver, and Montreal. Opportunities abound in software development, artificial intelligence, cybersecurity, and clean technology.

- Natural Resources: The country is rich in natural resources, including oil, gas, minerals, and forestry. Entrepreneurs can explore opportunities in sustainable resource management and related technologies.

- Healthcare and Life Sciences: With an aging population and a focus on health and wellness, there are opportunities in areas such as telemedicine, biotechnology, and medical devices.

- Tourism and Hospitality: Canada's breathtaking landscapes and cultural attractions make it a popular tourist destination. Entrepreneurs can tap into the hospitality industry through accommodation services, tour operators, and eco-tourism ventures.

- Renewable Energy: As the world shifts toward sustainability, Canada offers opportunities in renewable energy sources like solar, wind, and hydroelectric power.

In conclusion, embarking on an entrepreneurial journey in Canada can be rewarding and promising. Understanding the business landscape, recognizing the benefits and challenges, and identifying key industries and opportunities will set the stage for success. With the right planning, vision, and determination, entrepreneurs can flourish in this dynamic and welcoming market.

Chapter 2: Market Research and Idea Validation

One of the critical steps in starting a successful business in Canada is conducting thorough market research and validating your business idea. In this chapter, we will explore the importance of market research, methods for identifying business opportunities, and the process of evaluating the feasibility of your business idea by understanding customer needs and preferences.

2.1 The Importance of Market Research

Market research is the foundation of a well-informed business strategy. It involves gathering and analyzing data about the target market, industry trends, competition, and customer behavior. By conducting market research, entrepreneurs gain valuable insights that can shape their business decisions and enhance their chances of success. Some key reasons why market research is essential include:

- Identifying Opportunities: Market research helps entrepreneurs identify gaps in the market, unmet needs, and emerging trends that can be turned into business opportunities.

- Reducing Risk: Understanding the market landscape and customer preferences helps mitigate potential risks and uncertainties associated with starting a business.

- Targeting the Right Audience: Market research enables entrepreneurs to define their target audience accurately and tailor their products or services to meet customer demands.

- Competitive Analysis: Assessing competitors' strengths and weaknesses allows entrepreneurs to position their business effectively and create a unique value proposition.

- Making Informed Decisions: With data-driven insights, entrepreneurs can make informed decisions on pricing, marketing strategies, and product development.

2.2 Conducting Market Research to Identify Business Opportunities

To identify business opportunities through market research, entrepreneurs can follow these steps:

- Defining the Research Objective: Clearly define the goals of your market research. Are you looking for new product ideas, evaluating demand for a particular service, or exploring a niche market?

- Desk Research: Gather existing information and data from various sources, such as industry reports, government statistics, and online databases. This step can provide a broad overview of the market and its potential.

- Surveys and Questionnaires: Design and conduct surveys to collect feedback directly from potential customers. Online surveys, focus groups, or one-on-one interviews can help understand consumer preferences and pain points.

- Analyzing Competitors: Study your competitors' products, pricing, marketing strategies, and customer reviews. Identify gaps in the market that your business can address more effectively.

- Observing Trends: Keep an eye on industry trends, technological advancements, and changes in consumer behavior. Being aware of emerging trends can open new opportunities for your business.

- Exploring Demographics: Understand the demographics and psychographics of your target audience. Analyzing factors such as age, income, interests, and buying behavior can refine your business approach.

2.3 Evaluating the Feasibility of Your Business Idea

Market research alone is not sufficient; entrepreneurs must also evaluate the feasibility of their business idea. Here are some steps to assess whether your business concept is viable:

- Target Market Demand: Determine if there is sufficient demand for your product or service in the market. Validate whether customers are willing to pay for what you offer.

- Unique Value Proposition: Identify what sets your business apart from competitors and how it addresses customer needs better than existing solutions.

- Cost and Revenue Projections: Create financial projections that estimate startup costs, ongoing expenses, and potential revenue streams. Ensure that your business can generate profits and remain financially sustainable.

- Resource Availability: Assess the resources, skills, and expertise needed to run the business successfully. Consider if you have access to the necessary capital, workforce, and technology.

- Legal and Regulatory Compliance: Understand the legal and regulatory requirements relevant to your business. Ensure that you can meet all necessary obligations without significant hurdles.

2.4 Understanding Customer Needs and Preferences

Understanding your target customers is fundamental to delivering products or services that resonate with them. Here are ways to gain insight into customer needs and preferences:

- Persona Development: Create customer personas representing your ideal customers. Consider their demographics, preferences, pain points, and motivations.

- Surveys and Feedback: Continuously gather feedback from customers to understand their satisfaction levels and identify areas for improvement.

- Social Listening: Monitor social media platforms and online reviews to gauge customer sentiment about your brand and products.

- Prototype Testing: If possible, create prototypes or minimum viable products (MVPs) and test them with a select group of potential customers. Their feedback can shape your final offering.

- Continuous Adaptation: Stay agile and adapt your products or services based on changing customer needs and preferences over time.

In conclusion, market research and idea validation are critical steps in the entrepreneurial journey. By thoroughly understanding the market, identifying business opportunities, and evaluating the feasibility of your business idea while keeping customer needs in mind, you can lay a strong foundation for success. Market research empowers entrepreneurs to make informed decisions, minimize risks, and create offerings that resonate with their target audience in the dynamic and competitive Canadian market.

Chapter 3: Legal and Regulatory Considerations

Starting a business in Canada involves navigating various legal and regulatory considerations. Understanding the different business structures, registering your business, obtaining necessary licenses and permits, and ensuring compliance with tax obligations are essential steps for any aspiring entrepreneur. In this chapter, we will delve into these crucial aspects to help you establish a solid legal foundation for your business.

3.1 Business Structures in Canada

When starting a business in Canada, you must choose a suitable business structure that aligns with your goals, liability preferences, and tax implications. The common types of business structures in Canada include:

1. Sole Proprietorship: This is the simplest and most common form of business structure. The business is owned and operated by a single individual, making that person personally liable for the business's debts and obligations.

2. Partnership: A partnership involves two or more individuals who share ownership and management responsibilities. In a general partnership, each partner is personally liable for the business's debts. In a limited partnership, there are general partners who have full liability and limited partners with limited liability.

3. Corporation: A corporation is a separate legal entity from its owners (shareholders). It offers limited liability protection to shareholders, meaning their personal assets are generally protected from the company's debts and liabilities.

4. Cooperative: A cooperative is an organization owned and operated by its members, who use its products or services. Profits are distributed among members based on their contributions to the cooperative.

Each business structure has its advantages and disadvantages, and the right choice depends on factors such as the size of the business, liability concerns, tax considerations, and long-term goals.

3.2 Registering Your Business and Obtaining Necessary Licenses and Permits

Registering your business is a crucial step in establishing its legal identity. The process may vary depending on the business structure and the province or territory where you plan to operate. Here are general steps to register your business:

1. Choose a Business Name: Select a unique and appropriate name for your business. Check if the name is available and meets the naming requirements in your province or territory.

2. Business Registration: Register your business with the appropriate provincial or territorial authorities. For sole proprietorships and partnerships, registration is often done at the provincial level. Corporations are registered federally or provincially, depending on the scope of your business.

3. Obtain Business Permits and Licenses: Depending on the nature of your business, you may need specific permits or licenses to operate legally. These requirements vary by industry and location, so it's essential to research and obtain the necessary permits before starting operations.

4. Business Number (BN): If your business is going to have employees or deal with certain government agencies, you will need to obtain a Business Number (BN) from the Canada Revenue Agency (CRA).

5. Goods and Services Tax (GST)/Harmonized Sales Tax (HST) Registration: If your business's annual revenue is above a certain threshold, you may need to register for GST/HST, which is a value-added tax.

6. Employer Identification Number (EIN): If your business is incorporated and will hire employees, you will need an Employer Identification Number (EIN) for tax and payroll purposes.

3.3 Understanding Tax Obligations and Compliance

As a business owner in Canada, you must comply with various tax obligations at the federal, provincial, and municipal levels. Here are some essential tax considerations:

1. Income Tax: Businesses in Canada are subject to federal and provincial income taxes based on their profits. Corporations are taxed at corporate tax rates, while sole proprietors and partnerships report business income on their personal tax returns.

2. Goods and Services Tax (GST)/Harmonized Sales Tax (HST): If your business is registered for GST/HST, you will need to collect and remit these taxes on eligible sales. The rates vary by province.

3. Payroll Taxes: If you have employees, you must withhold income tax, Canada Pension Plan (CPP) contributions, and Employment Insurance (EI) premiums from their wages and remit them to the appropriate government agencies.

4. Provincial Taxes: Some provinces have additional taxes and levies that businesses must be aware of, such as provincial sales taxes or payroll taxes.

5. Tax Filing: Businesses must file various tax returns, such as corporate income tax returns, GST/HST returns, and payroll-related filings, on time to avoid penalties and interest.

It's essential to keep accurate financial records and work with an accountant or tax professional to ensure compliance with tax laws and optimize your tax position.

In conclusion, understanding the legal and regulatory landscape in Canada is vital for starting and running a successful business.

Carefully selecting the appropriate business structure, registering your business, obtaining necessary licenses and permits, and complying with tax obligations will provide a solid legal foundation for your entrepreneurial venture. Taking these steps early on will help you focus on growing your business with confidence and peace of mind.

Chapter 4: Crafting a Solid Business Plan

A well-crafted business plan is an essential roadmap for your entrepreneurial journey in Canada. It serves as a comprehensive blueprint that outlines your business objectives, strategies, and financial projections. In this chapter, we will explore the key elements of a successful business plan, including creating a vision, mission, and business goals, as well as financial projections and budgeting.

4.1 Elements of a Successful Business Plan

A successful business plan typically includes the following key elements:

1. Executive Summary: A concise overview of your business idea, highlighting the main points of the plan. It should be compelling and engaging, encouraging readers to delve into the details.

2. Company Description: Describe your business, its history (if applicable), its legal structure, and its location. Explain your products or services and the unique value proposition that sets your business apart from competitors.

3. Market Analysis: Conduct a thorough analysis of your target market, industry trends, and competitor landscape. Provide insights into customer demographics, preferences, and buying behavior.

4. Organizational Structure and Management: Describe the organizational structure of your business, including key roles and responsibilities. Introduce the management team and highlight their relevant experience and expertise.

5. Products or Services: Provide detailed information about your offerings, including features, benefits, and pricing. Explain how your products or services address customer needs and solve their pain points.

6. Sales and Marketing Strategy: Outline your sales and marketing plan, including the channels you'll use to reach your target audience, promotional strategies, and customer acquisition tactics.

7. Funding Request (if applicable): If you're seeking external funding, clearly state the amount you need and how you plan to use it. Provide a breakdown of how the funds will be allocated to different aspects of the business.

8. Financial Projections: Present financial forecasts, including sales projections, expenses, and cash flow estimates for the next three to five years. Include assumptions and explanations for your projections.

9. Risk Analysis: Identify potential risks and challenges your business may face, along with mitigation strategies to minimize their impact.

10. Appendices: Include any additional information that supports your business plan, such as market research data, legal documents, and resumes of key team members.

4.2 Creating a Vision, Mission, and Business Goals

A clear vision, mission, and well-defined goals are foundational elements of your business plan. They provide a sense of direction and purpose, guiding your decisions and actions. Here's how to craft these essential components:

1. Vision Statement: Your vision statement is a concise description of what you aspire to achieve in the long term. It should be inspirational and capture the essence of your business's ultimate impact or success.

2. Mission Statement: Your mission statement outlines your business's purpose, core values, and the value it brings to customers. It should articulate why your business exists and what

it aims to accomplish.

3. Business Goals: Set specific, measurable, achievable, relevant, and time-bound (SMART) goals for your business. These goals should align with your vision and mission and serve as milestones to track your progress.

Ensure that your vision, mission, and goals are communicated clearly throughout your business plan, reflecting a strong sense of purpose and guiding principles that resonate with stakeholders.

4.3 Financial Projections and Budgeting

Financial projections and budgeting are crucial components of your business plan, providing a realistic outlook on your business's financial performance. Here's how to approach this section:

1. Sales Projections: Estimate your sales revenue based on market research, pricing strategies, and anticipated customer demand.

2. Expense Projections: Forecast your operating expenses, including costs related to production, marketing, staffing, and overhead.

3. Cash Flow Analysis: Analyze your expected cash inflows and outflows over a specific period. Ensure that your business maintains positive cash flow to sustain operations.

4. Break-Even Analysis: Determine the point at which your business's total revenue equals its total expenses, signaling the point of profitability.

5. Budgeting: Develop a detailed budget that aligns with your financial projections. This will help you allocate resources effectively and track performance against your plan.

Regularly review and update your financial projections and budget as your business progresses. This allows you to adapt to changing market conditions and make informed financial decisions.

In conclusion, crafting a solid business plan is a critical step in building a successful business in Canada. The plan should encompass key elements such as a compelling executive summary, comprehensive market analysis, and a clear vision, mission, and business goals. Additionally, well-structured financial projections and budgeting provide a realistic outlook on your business's financial performance. A meticulously crafted business plan not only serves as a roadmap for your business but also communicates your vision and strategy to potential investors, partners, and stakeholders, increasing your chances of success in the competitive Canadian market.

Chapter 5: Financing Your Business

One of the critical aspects of starting and growing a successful business in Canada is securing the necessary funds to support your venture. In this chapter, we will explore various funding options available to entrepreneurs, including loans, grants, venture capital, and angel investors. Additionally, we will discuss how to prepare a compelling pitch to attract investors and the importance of managing personal finances during the early stages of your business.

5.1 Exploring Funding Options

Securing adequate funding is essential for turning your business idea into a reality. Here are some common funding options available to Canadian entrepreneurs:

1. Small Business Loans: Traditional bank loans are a common source of financing for businesses. These loans typically require collateral and have fixed interest rates and repayment terms.

2. Government Grants and Subsidies: The Canadian government offers various grants and subsidies to support startups and small businesses, especially those involved in research, innovation, and sustainable initiatives.

3. Venture Capital: Venture capital firms invest in high-potential startups in exchange for an ownership stake. They provide not only financial backing but also mentorship and industry connections.

4. Angel Investors: Angel investors are wealthy individuals who invest their personal funds in promising startups. They often seek a hands-on role in the business and provide guidance and networking opportunities.

5. Crowdfunding: Online crowdfunding platforms allow entrepreneurs to raise funds from a large number of individuals who contribute small amounts of money.

6. Bootstrapping: Self-funding, or bootstrapping, involves using personal savings or revenue generated by the business to finance its operations.

Each funding option has its advantages and considerations, and the choice depends on your business's needs, stage of development, and growth plans.

5.2 Preparing a Compelling Pitch for Investors

When seeking external funding, a well-prepared pitch is essential to capture the attention and interest of potential investors. Here are some tips for creating a compelling pitch:

1. Know Your Audience: Tailor your pitch to the specific interests and goals of the investors you are targeting. Understand their investment criteria and align your pitch accordingly.

2. Concise and Engaging: Keep your pitch concise and focused on the most critical aspects of your business. Clearly communicate your unique value proposition and what sets your business apart.

3. Address Market Opportunities: Clearly define the market opportunities and potential for growth in your industry. Provide data and market research to back up your claims.

4. Highlight the Team: Emphasize the skills and experience of your management team. Investors often consider the team's capabilities as a critical factor in their investment decision.

5. Financial Projections: Present realistic and well-supported financial projections that demonstrate your business's revenue potential and profitability.

6. Be Transparent: Be open and transparent about potential risks and challenges your business may face. Investors appreciate honesty and a clear plan for mitigating risks.

7. Practice and Refine: Practice your pitch with colleagues,

mentors, or advisors. Accept feedback and refine your presentation to make it as impactful as possible.

Remember that an effective pitch not only communicates your business idea but also showcases your passion, commitment, and confidence in making the business a success.

5.3 Managing Personal Finances during the Early Stages

In the early stages of your business, personal finances can be closely tied to its success. Here are some tips for managing your personal finances responsibly:

1. Establish a Budget: Create a personal budget to manage your living expenses and ensure that you can sustain yourself while your business grows.

2. Maintain an Emergency Fund: Set aside an emergency fund to cover unforeseen personal expenses and emergencies without relying solely on your business.

3. Separate Business and Personal Finances: Keep your business finances separate from your personal finances. Open a dedicated business bank account to track business transactions.

4. Limit Personal Guarantees: Be cautious about providing personal guarantees for business loans or credit. Explore alternative financing options that don't require personal guarantees whenever possible.

5. Seek Financial Advice: Consult with a financial advisor or accountant to manage your personal finances effectively and make informed decisions about investment and debt management.

6. Focus on Cash Flow: Pay close attention to your business's cash flow to ensure it can sustain your personal expenses and business operations.

Managing personal finances responsibly can reduce stress and provide a safety net as you navigate the challenges and uncertainties of entrepreneurship.

In conclusion, securing adequate funding and managing personal finances are crucial elements of launching and growing a successful business in Canada. Exploring various funding options, preparing a compelling pitch for investors, and being mindful of personal financial management are essential steps for entrepreneurs to take. With a solid financial foundation and effective funding strategies, you can focus on building and scaling your business in the dynamic Canadian market.

Chapter 6: Building a Strong Team

A strong and motivated team is the backbone of a successful business. As an entrepreneur in Canada, identifying key roles, hiring the right talent, fostering a positive company culture, promoting diversity, and ensuring compliance with employee rights and labor laws are critical aspects of building a cohesive and high-performing team. In this chapter, we will explore how to create a strong team that contributes to the growth and success of your business.

6.1 Identifying Key Roles and Hiring the Right Talent

Building a strong team begins with identifying key roles and hiring individuals who possess the right skills, experience, and values. Here are steps to help you in this process:

1. Assess Organizational Needs: Identify the roles essential for the smooth functioning of your business. Determine the specific skills and qualifications required for each position.

2. Write Clear Job Descriptions: Craft detailed job descriptions that outline responsibilities, qualifications, and expectations for each role. This will attract suitable candidates and provide a clear understanding of their future responsibilities.

3. Conduct Thorough Interviews: During the interview process, evaluate candidates not only based on their technical skills but also on their cultural fit and alignment with your business's values and vision.

4. Consider Diversity and Inclusion: Embrace diversity in your team by ensuring equal opportunities for individuals of different backgrounds, genders, and ethnicities. A diverse team can bring fresh perspectives and foster innovation.

5. Onboarding and Training: Once you've hired the right talent, invest in their onboarding and continuous training to ensure they have the tools and knowledge needed to excel in their roles.

6.2 Creating a Positive Company Culture and Promoting Diversity

A positive company culture plays a significant role in attracting and retaining top talent. Here's how to cultivate a positive work environment:

1. Lead by Example: As a leader, embody the values and principles you want your team to follow. Demonstrate respect, transparency, and integrity in your actions.

2. Foster Open Communication: Encourage open and honest communication among team members. Create channels for feedback and actively listen to your employees' concerns and suggestions.

3. Recognize and Reward Success: Celebrate individual and team achievements. Recognizing employees' efforts boosts morale and motivates them to excel.

4. Promote Work-Life Balance: Encourage work-life balance to prevent burnout and promote overall well-being among your team members.

5. Embrace Flexibility: Consider offering flexible work arrangements, such as remote work or flexible hours, to accommodate diverse employee needs.

6. Celebrate Diversity: Embrace diversity and create an inclusive environment where all team members feel valued and respected for their unique contributions.

6.3 Employee Rights and Labor Laws in Canada

As an employer in Canada, it's crucial to understand and comply with employee rights and labor laws to avoid legal issues. Some key labor laws and rights in Canada include:

1. Employment Standards: Employment standards vary by

province or territory but typically cover areas such as minimum wage, working hours, overtime pay, vacation entitlements, and termination notice.

2. Workplace Health and Safety: Employers must provide a safe and healthy work environment and comply with health and safety regulations.

3. Human Rights Legislation: Businesses are prohibited from discriminating against employees based on protected characteristics such as race, gender, religion, and disability.

4. Employment Contracts: Having written employment contracts that outline terms of employment, including compensation, benefits, and job expectations, can help prevent misunderstandings.

5. Termination and Severance: Terminating an employee's employment must follow the appropriate procedures and, in some cases, may require providing severance pay.

6. Privacy Laws: Ensure that you comply with privacy laws when handling employees' personal information.

Stay informed about changes in labor laws and seek legal advice to ensure compliance with relevant employment regulations.

In conclusion, building a strong team is essential for the success of your business in Canada. Identifying key roles and hiring the right talent, cultivating a positive company culture that promotes diversity and inclusion, and understanding and adhering to employee rights and labor laws are critical steps in creating a cohesive and motivated team. By investing in your team and providing a supportive work environment, you can attract and retain top talent, fostering a culture of growth, innovation, and success within your organization.

Chapter 7: Setting Up Your Business Location

The location of your business plays a significant role in its success. Whether you opt for a physical office space or embrace remote work and virtual office options, choosing the right setup can impact your business operations, accessibility, and overall productivity. In this chapter, we will explore the considerations involved in selecting the optimal business location, leasing agreements and commercial property considerations, as well as the benefits of remote work and virtual office solutions.

7.1 Choosing the Right Location for Your Business

Selecting the right location for your business is crucial as it can influence factors such as visibility, accessibility, customer reach, and proximity to suppliers and partners. Here are some key considerations:

1. Target Market Proximity: Consider the proximity to your target market and customers. Being located close to your target audience can increase foot traffic and brand exposure.

2. Competitor Analysis: Research the locations of your competitors and assess how your business can differentiate itself in the same area or explore untapped markets in other regions.

3. Accessibility and Transportation: Ensure that your chosen location is easily accessible to customers, employees, and suppliers. Proximity to public transportation and major roads can be advantageous.

4. Zoning and Regulations: Check local zoning regulations and ensure that your business is allowed to operate in your chosen location. Obtain necessary permits and licenses accordingly.

5. Amenities and Infrastructure: Consider the availability of amenities such as parking, restaurants, and retail outlets, which can enhance the convenience of your business location.

6. Cost and Affordability: Evaluate the cost of renting or owning a space in different areas, taking into account your budget and business financials.

7.2 Leasing Agreements and Commercial Property Considerations

If you decide to set up a physical office or retail space, navigating leasing agreements and commercial property considerations is essential. Here are some key factors to consider:

1. Lease Terms and Negotiation: Review lease terms carefully, including rent, lease duration, renewal options, and any additional costs or responsibilities. Negotiate terms that align with your business needs.

2. Space Requirements: Determine the size and layout of the space required to accommodate your business operations, employees, and future growth.

3. Lease Flexibility: Consider the flexibility of the lease in case you need to expand or downsize your business in the future.

4. Maintenance and Repairs: Clarify who is responsible for maintenance, repairs, and improvements to the property, and ensure it aligns with your budget and preferences.

5. Legal Advice: Seek legal advice before signing a lease to understand your rights and obligations fully.

7.3 Remote Work and Virtual Office Options

In recent years, remote work and virtual office options have gained popularity, offering businesses flexibility and cost savings. Here are the benefits of considering remote work and virtual office solutions:

1. Cost Savings: Remote work and virtual offices can significantly reduce overhead costs, including rent, utilities, and office supplies.

2. Talent Pool: Embracing remote work allows you to access a broader talent pool beyond your local area, potentially attracting skilled employees from different regions.

3. Work-Life Balance: Remote work provides employees with increased flexibility, contributing to improved work-life balance and job satisfaction.

4. Technology and Connectivity: Advancements in technology enable seamless collaboration and communication among remote teams.

5. Scalability: Virtual office solutions can easily adapt to your business's growth or downsizing needs without the constraints of a physical location.

Before implementing remote work arrangements, establish clear guidelines, communication protocols, and performance expectations to ensure smooth operations and maintain team cohesion.

In conclusion, choosing the right business location involves careful consideration of factors such as proximity to the target market, competitor analysis, accessibility, and amenities. Whether you opt for a physical office space with leasing agreements or embrace remote work and virtual office options, each choice comes with its own benefits and considerations. By aligning your business location with your goals, budget, and desired work environment, you can create a setup that fosters productivity, innovation, and success in the competitive Canadian market.

Chapter 8: Developing a Marketing Strategy

A well-crafted marketing strategy is essential for attracting customers, building brand awareness, and driving business growth. In this chapter, we will explore the steps involved in developing a successful marketing strategy for your business in Canada, including understanding your target market and customer segmentation, leveraging online and offline marketing channels, and implementing brand awareness and customer acquisition techniques.

8.1 Understanding Your Target Market and Customer Segmentation

Understanding your target market is the foundation of an effective marketing strategy. Here are the steps to gain insight into your audience and segment your customers:

1. Market Research: Conduct thorough market research to identify your target market's preferences, needs, and pain points. Analyze demographics, behavior patterns, and purchasing habits.

2. Customer Personas: Create detailed customer personas representing your ideal customers. These personas should encompass their characteristics, interests, challenges, and motivations.

3. Customer Segmentation: Segment your customers into groups based on shared characteristics and behaviors. This allows you to tailor marketing messages to specific audience segments effectively.

4. Value Proposition: Develop a clear and compelling value proposition that communicates how your products or services address your target market's needs and offer unique benefits.

8.2 Online and Offline Marketing Channels in Canada

In today's digital age, a successful marketing strategy involves a combination of online and offline channels to reach a broader audience. Here are popular marketing channels in Canada:

1. Website and SEO: Establish a professional website that showcases your brand and offerings. Implement search engine optimization (SEO) to improve your website's visibility in search results.

2. Social Media: Leverage popular social media platforms to engage with your target audience, share valuable content, and build brand loyalty.

3. Content Marketing: Create valuable and relevant content, such as blogs, articles, videos, and infographics, to attract and retain customers.

4. Email Marketing: Build an email list and use email marketing campaigns to nurture leads, promote products, and keep customers informed.

5. Pay-Per-Click (PPC) Advertising: Use online advertising platforms, such as Google Ads and social media ads, to target specific audiences and drive website traffic.

6. Influencer Marketing: Collaborate with influencers in your industry to reach a wider audience and gain credibility.

7. Events and Networking: Participate in industry events, conferences, and local networking opportunities to connect with potential customers and partners offline.

8.3 Building Brand Awareness and Customer Acquisition Techniques

Building brand awareness is crucial for gaining recognition and trust in the market. Here are techniques to enhance your brand presence and acquire customers:

1. Consistent Branding: Develop a consistent brand identity, including logos, colors, and messaging, to create a cohesive and

recognizable brand image.

2. Content Marketing: Share valuable content that showcases your expertise and provides solutions to your audience's problems.

3. Social Media Engagement: Engage with your audience on social media, respond to comments and messages, and build a community around your brand.

4. Referral Programs: Encourage satisfied customers to refer friends and family to your business with referral incentives.

5. Free Trials and Demos: Offer free trials or demos of your products or services to allow potential customers to experience their value firsthand.

6. Discounts and Promotions: Use limited-time discounts and promotions to create a sense of urgency and encourage customer acquisition.

7. Customer Reviews and Testimonials: Showcase positive customer reviews and testimonials to build trust and credibility with potential customers.

8. Collaborations and Partnerships: Partner with complementary businesses or organizations to expand your reach and tap into new customer segments.

Monitor the effectiveness of your marketing efforts through analytics and data tracking. Continuously analyze and refine your marketing strategy based on performance metrics to optimize results.

In conclusion, a well-developed marketing strategy is essential for business success in Canada. Understanding your target market and customer segmentation, leveraging online and offline marketing channels, and implementing brand awareness and customer acquisition techniques are key steps to attract and retain customers in the competitive Canadian market. By continuously adapting and refining your marketing approach based on performance metrics, you can build a strong brand presence, drive business growth, and stay ahead of the competition.

Chapter 9: Creating a Strong Online Presence

In the digital age, establishing a strong online presence is essential for business success. A robust online presence enables you to reach a broader audience, engage with potential customers, and drive business growth. In this chapter, we will explore the key steps to creating a strong online presence, including building and optimizing a business website, leveraging social media and content marketing, and utilizing e-commerce platforms and digital marketing tools.

9.1 Building and Optimizing a Business Website

A business website serves as the virtual storefront of your company and is often the first point of contact with potential customers. Here are steps to build and optimize an effective website:

1. Clear Branding: Ensure your website reflects your brand identity with consistent colors, logos, and messaging.

2. User-Friendly Design: Create a user-friendly and intuitive website layout that enables visitors to navigate easily and find the information they need.

3. Mobile Responsiveness: Optimize your website for mobile devices to provide a seamless experience for users on smartphones and tablets.

4. Engaging Content: Offer valuable and engaging content that showcases your products or services and provides solutions to your audience's problems.

5. Call-to-Action (CTA): Include clear and compelling calls-to-action to encourage visitors to take the desired actions, such as making a purchase or signing up for a newsletter.

6. Contact Information: Display your contact information prominently, making it easy for potential customers to get in

touch with you.

7. Search Engine Optimization (SEO): Implement SEO strategies to improve your website's visibility in search engine results, driving organic traffic to your site.

8. Website Analytics: Use website analytics tools to track visitor behavior and engagement, allowing you to make data-driven improvements.

9.2 Leveraging Social Media and Content Marketing

Social media and content marketing play a crucial role in building brand awareness and engaging with your audience. Here's how to leverage these platforms effectively:

1. Social Media Presence: Choose the social media platforms most relevant to your target audience, and maintain an active presence by sharing content, engaging with followers, and responding to comments.

2. Content Strategy: Develop a content marketing strategy that includes blogs, videos, infographics, and other valuable content that aligns with your audience's interests.

3. Consistency: Maintain consistency in your posting schedule and messaging to build brand recognition and trust.

4. Engaging Content: Create content that encourages interaction and sharing, fostering a sense of community around your brand.

5. Influencer Partnerships: Collaborate with influencers or industry experts to reach a broader audience and gain credibility.

6. Social Media Advertising: Use social media advertising to target specific audiences and promote your products or services effectively.

9.3 Utilizing E-commerce Platforms and Digital Marketing Tools

E-commerce platforms and digital marketing tools are essential for selling products online and reaching a wider audience. Here's how to make the most of these tools:

1. E-commerce Platform: Choose an e-commerce platform that suits your business needs and offers user-friendly shopping experiences for customers.

2. Product Listings: Create detailed and visually appealing product listings with high-quality images and compelling product descriptions.

3. Online Payments: Ensure that your e-commerce platform supports secure and seamless online payment methods for customer convenience.

4. Email Marketing: Utilize email marketing to nurture leads, inform customers about promotions, and drive sales.

5. Digital Advertising: Implement digital advertising campaigns, such as Google Ads and social media ads, to reach your target audience and drive website traffic.

6. Marketing Automation: Use marketing automation tools to streamline marketing tasks and deliver personalized content to your audience.

By leveraging these online platforms and tools effectively, you can enhance your online presence, engage with your audience, and drive sales, positioning your business for long-term success in the digital landscape.

In conclusion, creating a strong online presence is essential for business growth and success in the digital age. Building and optimizing a business website, leveraging social media and content marketing, and utilizing e-commerce platforms and digital marketing tools are key steps in establishing a robust online presence. By engaging with your audience, providing valuable content, and utilizing effective marketing strategies, you can reach a broader audience, build brand recognition, and drive business growth in the competitive online marketplace.

Chapter 10: Managing Finances and Accounting

Effective financial management and accounting are vital for the success and sustainability of your business in Canada. In this chapter, we will explore the steps involved in setting up a bookkeeping and accounting system, tracking expenses, revenue, and financial reports, and understanding Canadian financial regulations to ensure compliance and informed decision-making.

10.1 Setting up a Bookkeeping and Accounting System

Setting up a reliable bookkeeping and accounting system is essential for keeping track of your business's financial transactions and maintaining accurate records. Here are the key steps to establish an effective system:

1. Choose an Accounting Method: Decide on a suitable accounting method for your business—cash basis or accrual basis. The cash basis records transactions when money changes hands, while the accrual basis records transactions when they occur, regardless of cash flow.

2. Separate Business and Personal Finances: Maintain separate bank accounts and credit cards for your business and personal expenses to avoid mixing funds.

3. Select Accounting Software: Consider using accounting software that aligns with your business needs and allows you to automate financial tasks, track income and expenses, and generate financial reports.

4. Hire a Professional: If you're unfamiliar with accounting practices, consider hiring an accountant or bookkeeper to set up the system and manage your financial records.

10.2 Tracking Expenses, Revenue, and Financial Reports

Accurate tracking of expenses, revenue, and financial reports is crucial for making informed business decisions and assessing your business's financial health. Here's how to stay on top of your financial records:

1. Track Income and Expenses: Record all business income and expenses diligently. Keep receipts, invoices, and transaction records organized and accessible.

2. Monitor Cash Flow: Regularly track your business's cash flow to understand how money flows in and out of your company.

3. Reconcile Bank Accounts: Reconcile your bank accounts regularly to ensure that your records match your actual bank balances.

4. Generate Financial Statements: Generate financial statements, such as income statements, balance sheets, and cash flow statements, to assess your business's performance and financial position.

5. Budgeting: Develop a budget for your business to plan and allocate resources effectively.

6. Regular Reviews: Review your financial reports regularly to identify trends, spot areas for improvement, and make informed financial decisions.

10.3 Understanding Canadian Financial Regulations

As a business owner in Canada, it's crucial to understand and comply with the financial regulations that govern your operations. Here are some key regulations to be aware of:

1. Goods and Services Tax (GST)/Harmonized Sales Tax (HST): If your business is registered for GST/HST, you must collect and remit these taxes on eligible sales.

2. Corporate Income Tax: Corporations are subject to federal and provincial income taxes based on their profits.

3. Payroll Taxes: If you have employees, you must withhold

income tax, Canada Pension Plan (CPP) contributions, and Employment Insurance (EI) premiums from their wages and remit them to the appropriate government agencies.

4. Financial Reporting Requirements: Ensure that your financial reports comply with the Generally Accepted Accounting Principles (GAAP) and other relevant regulations.

5. Record Keeping: Maintain accurate financial records and keep them accessible for inspection by tax authorities, if required.

6. Industry-Specific Regulations: Some industries may have specific financial regulations and reporting requirements. Research and comply with any sector-specific rules applicable to your business.

7. Seek Professional Advice: Consult with an accountant or financial advisor to ensure you are in compliance with all relevant financial regulations and receive advice tailored to your business's unique needs.

In conclusion, effective financial management and accounting are essential for the success and growth of your business in Canada. Setting up a bookkeeping and accounting system, tracking income and expenses, generating financial reports, and understanding Canadian financial regulations are key steps to maintain financial health, make informed decisions, and comply with legal requirements. By prioritizing financial management, you can position your business for long-term success and navigate the complexities of the Canadian financial landscape with confidence.

Chapter 11: Navigating Government Support and Incentive Programs

As an entrepreneur in Canada, tapping into government support and incentive programs can provide valuable resources and financial assistance to help your startup or small business thrive. In this chapter, we will explore how to identify government programs, grants, subsidies, and tax incentives available in Canada, and the benefits of engaging with business development organizations.

11.1 Identifying Government Programs for Startups and Small Businesses

The Canadian government offers a range of programs and initiatives to support startups and small businesses across various industries. These programs aim to foster innovation, growth, and job creation. Here's how to identify relevant government support:

1. Government Websites: Check official government websites at the federal, provincial, and municipal levels to find information on available programs.

2. Business Development Centers: Reach out to local business development centers or chambers of commerce, which often have information on government support programs.

3. Industry Associations: Industry-specific associations may have resources and information on government programs relevant to your sector.

4. Business Advisors: Consult with business advisors, accountants, or lawyers who can provide insights into available government incentives.

11.2 Grants, Subsidies, and Tax Incentives Available in Canada

Government grants, subsidies, and tax incentives can provide financial assistance and cost savings for your business. Here are some common types of incentives available in Canada:

1. Research and Development (R&D) Grants: Grants to support innovative research and development projects that can lead to new products or processes.

2. Hiring and Training Incentives: Subsidies to encourage hiring new employees or providing training for existing staff.

3. Export and Market Development Programs: Grants and support for businesses looking to expand into international markets.

4. Green Initiatives and Sustainability Programs: Incentives to promote environmentally friendly practices and sustainable business operations.

5. Tax Credits and Deductions: Various tax credits and deductions are available for eligible businesses, such as the Scientific Research and Experimental Development (SR&ED) Tax Incentive Program.

6. Startup Support: Many provinces and municipalities offer specific programs tailored to support early-stage startups.

It's essential to carefully review the eligibility criteria and application process for each incentive and ensure you meet the requirements before applying.

11.3 Engaging with Business Development Organizations

Business development organizations play a crucial role in supporting entrepreneurs and small businesses. Engaging with these organizations can provide valuable networking opportunities, mentorship, and access to resources. Here's how to make the most of these connections:

1. Local Chambers of Commerce: Join your local chamber of commerce to connect with other business owners, participate in networking events, and stay updated on relevant programs and incentives.

2. Incubators and Accelerators: Consider joining startup incubators or accelerators that offer mentorship, funding opportunities, and access to a supportive entrepreneurial community.

3. Trade Associations: Join trade associations related to your industry to gain industry-specific insights, attend conferences, and access specialized resources.

4. Networking Events: Attend networking events, workshops, and seminars organized by business development organizations to build connections and stay informed about industry trends.

5. Government Agencies: Engage with government agencies responsible for economic development and business support to learn about available programs and initiatives.

By actively engaging with business development organizations, you can expand your network, gain valuable advice, and discover additional opportunities for growth and support.

In conclusion, navigating government support and incentive programs can provide significant advantages for your startup or small business in Canada. By identifying relevant government programs, grants, subsidies, and tax incentives, you can access valuable resources to support your business's growth and innovation. Additionally, engaging with business development organizations offers access to networking opportunities, mentorship, and specialized support. Be proactive in exploring these avenues to maximize the benefits of government support and enhance your business's chances of success in the Canadian market.

Chapter 12: Protecting Your Intellectual Property

Intellectual property (IP) is a valuable asset for businesses, and safeguarding it is crucial to prevent unauthorized use and ensure your competitive advantage. In this chapter, we will explore the importance of understanding intellectual property rights in Canada, the registration processes for trademarks, patents, and copyrights, as well as strategies for enforcing and defending your intellectual property.

12.1 Understanding Intellectual Property Rights in Canada

Intellectual property encompasses intangible creations of the mind, such as inventions, brands, designs, and artistic works. Understanding your intellectual property rights is the first step in protecting your innovations and original creations. In Canada, the main types of intellectual property rights include:

1. Trademarks: Protect your brand names, logos, and slogans that distinguish your goods or services from others in the market.

2. Patents: Safeguard your inventions or novel processes, granting you exclusive rights to produce, use, or sell the patented invention for a limited time.

3. Copyrights: Protect your original literary, artistic, and creative works, such as books, music, artwork, and software.

4. Industrial Designs: Secure the visual appearance of a product or its ornamentation.

5. Trade Secrets: Keep confidential information, such as formulas, recipes, or customer lists, secret to gain a competitive edge.

12.2 Trademarks, Patents, and Copyrights Registration

Registering your trademarks, patents, and copyrights provides legal protection and establishes your exclusive rights. Here's an overview of the registration processes:

1. Trademarks: Register your trademarks with the Canadian Intellectual Property Office (CIPO). The registration process involves a thorough examination to ensure your trademark meets the necessary requirements.

2. Patents: File a patent application with CIPO, describing the invention's novelty, non-obviousness, and utility. The application undergoes examination before being granted.

3. Copyrights: Although copyrights automatically exist upon creating original works, you can register your copyrights with the Canadian Intellectual Property Office (CIPO) to obtain additional legal benefits.

Consult with an intellectual property lawyer or agent to ensure your applications meet the required standards and navigate the registration process smoothly.

12.3 Enforcing and Defending Your Intellectual Property

Protecting your intellectual property does not end with registration. Vigilance and prompt action are necessary to enforce and defend your rights against infringement. Here are strategies to safeguard your intellectual property:

1. Monitor Your IP: Regularly monitor the market and online platforms for unauthorized use of your trademarks or copyrighted material.

2. Cease and Desist: If you discover infringement, send a cease and desist letter to the infringing party, requesting them to stop using your intellectual property.

3. Seek Legal Action: If the infringement persists, consult with an intellectual property lawyer to explore legal actions, such as filing a lawsuit for damages or seeking an injunction.

4. Licensing Agreements: Consider licensing your intellectual property to others under specific terms and conditions, which can

generate revenue while maintaining control over its use.

5. International Protection: If your business operates internationally, explore options to protect your intellectual property in other countries through international treaties and registrations.

6. Prior Art Searches: Before investing in new inventions, conduct prior art searches to identify existing patents that may pose obstacles to your patent application.

Taking proactive steps to enforce and defend your intellectual property is essential to preserve your competitive advantage, brand reputation, and market position.

In conclusion, understanding intellectual property rights, registering trademarks, patents, and copyrights, and adopting effective enforcement and defense strategies are critical for protecting your business's valuable innovations and creative works. By securing intellectual property rights and actively monitoring and defending them, you can safeguard your competitive edge, maintain brand integrity, and enhance the long-term success of your business in Canada.

Chapter 13: Managing Risk and Insurance

Effective risk management and insurance play a crucial role in protecting your business from unforeseen events and potential liabilities. In this chapter, we will explore the types of business insurance required in Canada, risk assessment and mitigation strategies, and how to protect your business against liability and unexpected events.

13.1 Types of Business Insurance Required in Canada

Having the right insurance coverage is essential to safeguard your business from various risks. While the specific insurance needs may vary depending on your industry and business structure, some common types of business insurance required in Canada include:

1. Commercial Property Insurance: Protects your business property, such as buildings, equipment, inventory, and furniture, against perils like fire, theft, and vandalism.

2. General Liability Insurance: Provides coverage for legal costs and financial liabilities arising from third-party injuries, property damage, or other incidents related to your business operations.

3. Professional Liability Insurance (Errors and Omissions Insurance): Essential for service-based businesses, it covers claims related to professional negligence, errors, or omissions in the services you provide.

4. Product Liability Insurance: Protects your business from claims resulting from injuries or damages caused by your products.

5. Cyber Liability Insurance: Provides coverage for losses resulting from data breaches, cyber-attacks, or unauthorized access to sensitive information.

6. Business Interruption Insurance: Helps cover the loss of income and ongoing expenses if your business operations are interrupted

due to covered perils.

7. Commercial Auto Insurance: Covers vehicles used for business purposes against accidents and damages.

8. Directors and Officers (D&O) Insurance: Protects the personal assets of directors and officers against legal actions related to their decisions and actions taken on behalf of the company.

Before purchasing insurance policies, assess your business risks and consult with an insurance professional to ensure you have adequate coverage for your specific needs.

13.2 Risk Assessment and Mitigation Strategies

Conducting a thorough risk assessment is crucial to identify potential threats to your business and develop mitigation strategies. Here's how to manage risks effectively:

1. Identify Risks: Identify internal and external risks that could impact your business, such as market changes, natural disasters, cybersecurity threats, and supply chain disruptions.

2. Assess Impact and Likelihood: Evaluate the potential impact and likelihood of each risk occurring to prioritize and address the most critical threats.

3. Develop Mitigation Plans: Create detailed risk mitigation plans that outline specific actions to reduce the impact of identified risks.

4. Contingency Planning: Develop contingency plans to address potential crises and ensure business continuity in case of unexpected events.

5. Training and Education: Train employees on risk management practices, cybersecurity protocols, and safety procedures to minimize potential risks caused by human error.

6. Regular Reviews: Regularly review and update your risk

assessment and mitigation plans to adapt to changing business conditions and emerging threats.

13.3 Protecting Against Liability and Unexpected Events

In addition to insurance and risk management strategies, implementing the following practices can further protect your business against liability and unexpected events:

1. Strong Contracts: Use well-drafted contracts with clear terms and conditions to establish legal agreements with clients, suppliers, and partners.

2. Safety Measures: Implement workplace safety measures to prevent accidents and reduce the risk of liability claims from employees and customers.

3. Document Retention: Maintain organized records and documentation related to business transactions, contracts, and financial transactions.

4. Legal Advice: Consult with legal counsel to ensure your business practices and contracts comply with applicable laws and regulations.

5. Business Continuity Planning: Develop a comprehensive business continuity plan to ensure your business can recover and resume operations in the event of a disaster.

6. Employee Training: Educate employees on security protocols, data protection, and customer privacy to minimize cybersecurity risks.

By taking proactive measures to manage risks, securing the right insurance coverage, and implementing protection strategies, you can fortify your business against liabilities and unexpected events, ensuring its resilience and long-term success in the Canadian market.

In conclusion, managing risk and insurance are essential aspects of ensuring the sustainability and growth of your business in Canada. Understanding the types of insurance required, conducting risk assessments, and implementing mitigation strategies can help protect your business from potential liabilities and unexpected events. By being proactive in managing risks and securing appropriate insurance coverage, you can strengthen your business's ability to withstand challenges and position it for continued success in the dynamic business environment.

Chapter 14: Scaling Your Business

Scaling your business is an exciting phase that involves expanding operations, exploring new markets, and forming strategic partnerships. In this chapter, we will explore strategies for growth and expansion, the opportunities in international markets and exporting, and the benefits of building partnerships and alliances to propel your business to new heights.

14.1 Strategies for Growth and Expansion

Scaling your business requires careful planning and execution. Here are effective strategies to achieve growth and expansion:

1. Market Diversification: Explore new customer segments or industries to reduce reliance on a single market and expand your customer base.

2. Product and Service Expansion: Introduce new products or services that complement your existing offerings or cater to emerging market needs.

3. Geographic Expansion: Consider opening new locations or entering different regions to reach a broader audience.

4. Online Expansion: Utilize e-commerce and digital marketing to expand your reach beyond local borders and tap into a global customer base.

5. Acquisitions and Mergers: Explore opportunities to acquire or merge with complementary businesses to gain a competitive edge and access new markets.

6. Franchising and Licensing: Consider franchising your business model or licensing your products to expand rapidly without significant capital investment.

7. Increase Production Capacity: Invest in technology, equipment, and infrastructure to meet growing demand.

8. Customer Retention: Focus on customer satisfaction and retention to create loyal advocates who refer your business to others.

14.2 Exploring International Markets and Exporting Opportunities

Expanding into international markets can offer significant growth opportunities for your business. Here's how to explore exporting and international expansion:

1. Market Research: Conduct thorough market research to identify potential international markets that align with your products or services.

2. Regulatory Compliance: Understand the import/export regulations, tariffs, and customs procedures of the target countries.

3. Adaptation: Tailor your products or marketing strategies to cater to the cultural preferences and needs of the international audience.

4. Distribution Channels: Establish reliable distribution channels, local partnerships, or use e-commerce platforms to reach customers in the target markets.

5. Trade Shows and Networking: Participate in international trade shows and networking events to connect with potential partners and customers.

6. Start with Strategic Countries: Begin by expanding into countries with a similar business environment and language to reduce barriers to entry.

14.3 Building Partnerships and Alliances

Forming strategic partnerships and alliances can accelerate your business growth and provide access to new resources. Here's how to build successful partnerships:

1. Identify Complementary Businesses: Look for businesses that offer products or services that complement yours without direct competition.

2. Shared Goals: Ensure that potential partners share similar values, goals, and commitment to the partnership's success.

3. Mutually Beneficial Agreements: Establish clear terms and conditions that benefit both parties and align with your long-term objectives.

4. Open Communication: Maintain transparent communication to foster trust and address any challenges that arise during the partnership.

5. Collaborative Marketing: Pool resources to conduct joint marketing campaigns or co-branding initiatives.

6. Strategic Alliances: Consider forming strategic alliances with industry leaders or influential organizations to gain credibility and exposure.

By employing these strategies for growth and expansion, exploring international markets and exporting opportunities, and building strategic partnerships and alliances, you can successfully scale your business and position it for sustained success and impact in the global market.

In conclusion, scaling your business is an exciting journey that requires careful planning and strategic decision-making. By implementing growth strategies, exploring international markets, and forming strategic partnerships, you can expand your business's reach, tap into new opportunities, and create a strong and sustainable presence in the competitive business landscape. Embrace innovation, stay adaptable, and continue to prioritize customer satisfaction to ensure a successful path towards scaling your business in Canada and beyond.

Chapter 15: Adapting to Technological Advancements

In the rapidly evolving business landscape, embracing technological advancements is crucial for staying competitive and ensuring business success. In this chapter, we will explore the importance of digital transformation for gaining a competitive advantage, the role of cloud computing, artificial intelligence, and automation in business, and the significance of cybersecurity and data protection measures to safeguard your business and customer information.

15.1 Embracing Digital Transformation for Competitive Advantage

Digital transformation involves integrating digital technologies into all aspects of your business, fundamentally changing how you operate and deliver value to customers. Here's why embracing digital transformation is essential for gaining a competitive advantage:

1. Improved Efficiency: Automation and digital tools streamline processes, reducing manual tasks and increasing operational efficiency.

2. Enhanced Customer Experience: Embracing technology allows you to provide personalized and seamless experiences to your customers, improving satisfaction and loyalty.

3. Data-Driven Decision Making: Digital transformation enables data collection and analysis, leading to better-informed strategic decisions.

4. Agility and Adaptability: Businesses that adopt digital practices can adapt quickly to changing market conditions and customer needs.

5. Access to New Markets: Technology can break geographical barriers, allowing businesses to expand their reach to new markets and demographics.

15.2 Cloud Computing, Artificial Intelligence, and Automation in Business

Cloud computing, artificial intelligence (AI), and automation are transformative technologies that offer significant benefits to businesses of all sizes:

1. Cloud Computing: Cloud services provide scalable and cost-effective solutions for storage, data management, and software access. It enables remote work, data accessibility, and disaster recovery.

2. Artificial Intelligence: AI applications can optimize various business processes, from customer service through chatbots to data analysis for personalized marketing strategies.

3. Automation: Automation streamlines repetitive tasks, reducing human errors and freeing up valuable resources for more strategic activities.

4. Internet of Things (IoT): IoT devices collect and share real-time data, enabling businesses to make data-driven decisions and offer proactive services.

5. Big Data Analytics: Analyzing large datasets allows businesses to gain insights into customer behavior, market trends, and operational performance.

By leveraging these technologies, businesses can achieve greater efficiency, innovation, and competitiveness in the digital era.

15.3 Cybersecurity and Data Protection Measures

As businesses become more technologically reliant, ensuring cybersecurity and data protection becomes paramount. Safeguarding sensitive information is essential to maintain trust with customers and protect your brand reputation. Here are crucial cybersecurity and data protection measures:

1. Secure Networks: Implement robust firewalls, encryption, and secure Wi-Fi networks to protect data from unauthorized access.

2. Employee Training: Educate employees on cybersecurity best practices, such as recognizing phishing emails and using strong passwords.

3. Regular Updates: Keep all software and systems up to date with the latest security patches to prevent vulnerabilities.

4. Data Backups: Regularly back up your data to a secure location to ensure business continuity in case of a cyber incident or data loss.

5. Privacy Compliance: Ensure compliance with relevant privacy regulations, such as the Personal Information Protection and Electronic Documents Act (PIPEDA) in Canada.

6. Incident Response Plan: Develop a comprehensive incident response plan to handle potential cyber threats effectively.

7. Third-Party Security: Ensure that third-party vendors and partners have adequate cybersecurity measures in place, especially if they have access to your data.

By prioritizing cybersecurity and data protection, you can safeguard your business, customer information, and intellectual property from cyber threats and data breaches.

In conclusion, adapting to technological advancements is a fundamental aspect of business growth and sustainability in the digital age. Embracing digital transformation for a competitive advantage, harnessing the power of cloud computing, artificial intelligence, and automation, and prioritizing cybersecurity and data protection measures are key to thriving in the dynamic and technologically-driven business landscape. By staying innovative and agile, you can position your business for success and create a robust and secure presence in the ever-evolving market.

Chapter 16: Building Customer Loyalty and Relations

Building strong customer loyalty and relationships is essential for the long-term success of your business. In this chapter, we will explore customer service best practices, creating loyalty programs and incentives, and managing feedback and handling customer complaints to foster trust, satisfaction, and loyalty among your customers.

16.1 Customer Service Best Practices

Exceptional customer service is the foundation of building strong customer loyalty. Here are some best practices to ensure an outstanding customer service experience:

1. Active Listening: Listen attentively to your customers' needs, concerns, and feedback to understand their perspective fully.

2. Timely Responses: Respond promptly to customer inquiries, whether through phone, email, or social media.

3. Personalization: Tailor interactions to individual customer preferences and needs, making them feel valued and understood.

4. Empathy and Courtesy: Approach customers with empathy and courtesy, even during challenging situations.

5. Knowledgeable Support: Provide well-trained and knowledgeable support staff who can address customer inquiries effectively.

6. Consistency: Maintain consistent service quality across all customer touchpoints to build trust and reliability.

7. Post-Sale Support: Offer post-sale support to assist customers with product or service-related issues.

8. Surveys and Feedback: Regularly collect customer feedback through surveys and actively use it to improve your offerings and service.

16.2 Creating Loyalty Programs and Incentives

Loyalty programs and incentives can incentivize repeat business and reinforce customer loyalty. Consider these strategies:

1. Rewards Programs: Implement a loyalty rewards program where customers earn points for purchases, which they can redeem for discounts, free products, or exclusive benefits.

2. VIP Memberships: Offer premium memberships with added perks, such as early access to new products or dedicated customer support.

3. Referral Incentives: Encourage customers to refer friends and family by offering rewards or discounts for successful referrals.

4. Birthday and Anniversary Offers: Recognize and appreciate customers by sending personalized offers on their birthdays or anniversaries with your business.

5. Exclusive Events and Previews: Host exclusive events or provide previews of new products or services for loyal customers.

6. Gamification: Introduce gamification elements, such as badges or achievement levels, to make loyalty programs engaging and fun.

16.3 Managing Feedback and Handling Customer Complaints

Customer feedback is a valuable resource for improvement, and handling complaints effectively can turn unhappy customers into loyal advocates. Here's how to manage feedback and complaints:

1. Encourage Feedback: Create multiple channels for customers to share feedback, such as online surveys, feedback forms, or social media platforms.

2. Acknowledge Complaints: Acknowledge customer complaints promptly and empathetically to show that their concerns are being taken seriously.

3. Apologize and Offer Solutions: Apologize for any inconvenience caused and provide appropriate solutions to address the issue.

4. Follow Up: Follow up with customers after resolving their complaints to ensure their satisfaction and show that you value their business.

5. Learn and Improve: Use feedback and complaint data to identify recurring issues and implement necessary improvements.

6. Empower Frontline Staff: Equip your frontline staff with the authority and resources to address customer complaints promptly.

By prioritizing excellent customer service, creating loyalty programs and incentives, and effectively managing feedback and complaints, you can build strong and lasting relationships with your customers. Satisfied and loyal customers are more likely to become brand advocates, driving new business through referrals and positive word-of-mouth, leading to sustainable growth and success for your business in Canada and beyond.

In conclusion, building customer loyalty and relationships is a vital aspect of business success. By prioritizing exceptional customer service, implementing loyalty programs and incentives, and effectively managing feedback and complaints, you can foster trust, satisfaction, and loyalty among your customers. Nurturing strong customer relationships will not only lead to increased customer retention but also open doors for new opportunities and growth in the competitive market. Always remember that happy customers are your best brand ambassadors and investing in customer loyalty will pay off in the long run.

Chapter 17: Sustainability and Corporate Social Responsibility

In today's business landscape, sustainability and corporate social responsibility (CSR) are essential components of a successful and ethical business. In this chapter, we will explore the importance of implementing environmentally friendly practices, engaging in social initiatives and community engagement, and upholding ethical business conduct to create a positive impact on society and the environment.

17.1 Implementing Environmentally Friendly Practices

As businesses play a significant role in environmental impact, adopting environmentally friendly practices is crucial for promoting sustainability and minimizing ecological footprints. Here are some key strategies for businesses to become more environmentally responsible:

1. Reduce, Reuse, Recycle: Implement waste reduction and recycling programs to minimize the environmental impact of your operations.

2. Energy Efficiency: Adopt energy-efficient technologies, lighting, and equipment to reduce energy consumption and carbon emissions.

3. Sustainable Procurement: Source products and materials from environmentally responsible suppliers who adhere to sustainable practices.

4. Green Transportation: Encourage the use of eco-friendly transportation options for employees and delivery services.

5. Sustainable Packaging: Opt for eco-friendly packaging materials that are biodegradable or recyclable.

6. Carbon Offsetting: Offset carbon emissions through initiatives such as tree planting or renewable energy projects.

By implementing environmentally friendly practices, businesses can contribute to environmental conservation and build a positive brand image as responsible corporate citizens.

17.2 Social Initiatives and Community Engagement

Corporate social responsibility extends beyond environmental considerations to social initiatives and community engagement. Engaging in social initiatives allows businesses to give back to the community and address social issues. Here are some ways to engage in CSR:

1. Philanthropy: Support charitable causes and nonprofit organizations through donations or sponsorships.

2. Employee Volunteering: Encourage employees to participate in volunteer programs and community service activities.

3. Education and Skill Development: Collaborate with educational institutions to provide skill development opportunities for students and aspiring professionals.

4. Local Community Support: Invest in community development projects, infrastructure improvements, and social welfare programs in the local area.

5. Diversity and Inclusion: Foster a diverse and inclusive workplace that values and promotes diversity in all aspects.

6. Human Rights and Fair Labor Practices: Ensure fair labor practices and human rights standards are maintained throughout the supply chain.

Engaging in social initiatives and community engagement not only benefits society but also enhances brand reputation and fosters goodwill among customers and stakeholders.

17.3 The Importance of Ethical Business Conduct

Ethical business conduct is a fundamental aspect of corporate social responsibility. Upholding ethical standards and values promotes trust and integrity within the organization and among stakeholders. Here's why ethical business conduct is crucial:

1. Trust and Reputation: Ethical businesses gain the trust and loyalty of customers, employees, and investors, leading to a positive reputation.

2. Employee Morale: Ethical practices create a positive work environment, fostering employee loyalty, and reducing turnover.

3. Legal Compliance: Adhering to ethical conduct ensures compliance with relevant laws and regulations.

4. Stakeholder Confidence: Ethical businesses earn the confidence of stakeholders, including shareholders, suppliers, and partners.

5. Long-Term Sustainability: Ethical conduct supports long-term business sustainability and growth.

Businesses should establish a code of ethics and conduct that outlines ethical standards and values, and ensure that employees at all levels are aware of and adhere to these principles.

In conclusion, sustainability and corporate social responsibility are integral to the success and ethical standing of modern businesses. By implementing environmentally friendly practices, engaging in social initiatives, and upholding ethical business conduct, businesses can make a positive impact on the environment, society, and their stakeholders. Embracing sustainability and CSR not only benefits society but also enhances brand reputation, employee satisfaction, and long-term business sustainability. As responsible corporate citizens, businesses have the power to create a meaningful difference in the world and contribute to a better and more sustainable future.

Chapter 18: Balancing Work-Life and Wellbeing

Entrepreneurship can be an exhilarating journey, but it often comes with high levels of stress and demanding work hours. In this chapter, we will explore strategies for overcoming entrepreneurial burnout, effective stress management techniques, and the importance of promoting wellness in the workplace to achieve a healthy work-life balance and overall wellbeing.

18.1 Overcoming Entrepreneurial Burnout

Entrepreneurial burnout is a state of physical, emotional, and mental exhaustion that can arise from the relentless demands of running a business. To overcome burnout, consider the following:

1. Self-Awareness: Recognize the signs of burnout, such as chronic fatigue, lack of motivation, or increased irritability.

2. Delegate and Prioritize: Delegate tasks to capable team members and focus on high-priority activities that align with your strengths.

3. Set Boundaries: Establish clear boundaries between work and personal life, and avoid overextending yourself.

4. Take Breaks: Schedule regular breaks throughout the day to recharge and prevent burnout.

5. Seek Support: Talk to trusted friends, family, or mentors about your feelings and challenges.

6. Practice Mindfulness: Engage in mindfulness practices, such as meditation or deep breathing, to reduce stress and increase focus.

18.2 Stress Management and Work-Life Balance

Effectively managing stress is essential for maintaining work-life balance and overall wellbeing. Consider these stress management techniques:

1. Time Management: Organize your tasks and prioritize activities to minimize stress and improve productivity.

2. Physical Activity: Engage in regular physical exercise to release endorphins and reduce stress levels.

3. Healthy Diet: Nourish your body with a balanced diet, as nutrition impacts mood and energy levels.

4. Restful Sleep: Prioritize quality sleep, as adequate rest is crucial for mental and physical rejuvenation.

5. Hobbies and Recreation: Make time for hobbies and activities you enjoy to relieve stress and promote relaxation.

6. Social Support: Stay connected with friends and family for emotional support and social interaction.

18.3 Promoting Wellness in the Workplace

Creating a wellness-oriented workplace fosters a healthy and positive environment for employees. Consider the following strategies:

1. Flexible Work Arrangements: Offer flexible work hours or remote work options to support work-life balance.

2. Employee Assistance Programs: Provide access to counseling and support services to help employees manage stress and personal challenges.

3. Health Initiatives: Implement health and wellness programs, such as yoga classes or fitness challenges, to encourage a healthy lifestyle.

4. Mental Health Support: Promote mental health awareness and provide resources for employees dealing with stress and mental health issues.

5. Ergonomic Workspace: Ensure that workstations are

ergonomically designed to reduce physical strain and discomfort.

6. Recognition and Appreciation: Recognize and appreciate employees' efforts and achievements to boost morale and job satisfaction.

By promoting wellness in the workplace, business owners can create a supportive and positive work environment, leading to higher employee engagement, productivity, and overall wellbeing.

In conclusion, maintaining a healthy work-life balance and prioritizing wellbeing is essential for entrepreneurs to sustain their passion and drive in the long run. Overcoming entrepreneurial burnout, adopting effective stress management techniques, and promoting workplace wellness contribute to a positive and sustainable work environment. By taking care of their physical and mental health, entrepreneurs can enhance their ability to make sound decisions, inspire their team, and lead their business to success. Remember, achieving work-life balance is a continuous journey, and investing in your wellbeing is a valuable investment in the overall success of your business and personal fulfillment.

Chapter 19: Exit Strategies and Succession Planning

As a business owner, planning for the future is crucial, including preparing for business succession or sale. In this chapter, we will explore the importance of exit strategies and succession planning, valuing your business, negotiation tactics, and ensuring a smooth transition for your business when the time comes to step down.

19.1 Preparing for Business Succession or Sale

Regardless of whether you plan to pass the business to a successor or sell it, having a clear exit strategy is essential. Consider the following steps in your preparation:

1. Define Your Goals: Determine your objectives for exiting the business. Are you looking for financial security, a legacy for your family, or a smooth transition for employees and customers?

2. Identify Successors: If you plan for succession, identify potential successors within the company or family who have the skills and capabilities to lead the business.

3. Seek Professional Advice: Consult with legal and financial advisors to understand the legal and tax implications of different exit strategies.

4. Plan Ahead: Start planning for your exit well in advance to allow time for the transition process and to maximize the value of your business.

19.2 Valuing Your Business and Negotiation Tactics

Determining the value of your business is a critical step in the exit process. Consider these factors to value your business:

1. Financial Performance: Assess your business's historical and projected financial performance.

2. Industry Comparables: Compare your business's financials and performance metrics with similar businesses in the industry.

3. Assets and Liabilities: Take inventory of your business's assets, liabilities, and intellectual property.

4. Market Conditions: Consider the current market conditions and industry trends that may impact your business's value.

When negotiating the sale or succession plan, be prepared to engage in open and transparent discussions with potential buyers or successors. Seek common ground and mutually beneficial outcomes to ensure a fair and successful negotiation process.

19.3 Ensuring a Smooth Transition for Your Business

A smooth transition is crucial to maintaining business continuity and preserving its value. Consider these steps to ensure a successful transition:

1. Train and Mentor Successors: Provide proper training and mentoring to the selected successor(s) to ensure a seamless transition of leadership.

2. Communicate with Stakeholders: Communicate the transition plan with employees, customers, suppliers, and other stakeholders to build confidence and trust.

3. Create a Succession Plan: Develop a comprehensive succession plan that outlines roles, responsibilities, and timelines for the transition.

4. Test the Transition Plan: Conduct trial runs or simulations of the transition plan to identify potential challenges and refine the process.

5. Stay Involved During Transition: Remain involved during the transition period to provide guidance and support to the new leadership.

6. Monitor Progress: Regularly monitor the progress of the transition and be prepared to address any unforeseen issues.

By carefully planning and executing the exit or succession strategy, you can ensure a smooth transition, preserve the value of your business, and leave a positive legacy.

In conclusion, exit strategies and succession planning are essential considerations for business owners to secure their legacy and prepare for the future. Whether you plan to pass the business to a successor or sell it, careful planning, valuing the business accurately, employing effective negotiation tactics, and ensuring a smooth transition are critical to a successful exit. By taking proactive steps and seeking professional advice, you can ensure that your business continues to thrive even after you step down and that your efforts and hard work leave a lasting impact on your business and its stakeholders.

Chapter 20: The Future of Canadian Entrepreneurship

As the Canadian entrepreneurial landscape continues to evolve, it presents exciting opportunities, innovations, and inspiring success stories. In this final chapter, we will explore the emerging trends and opportunities in the Canadian market, highlight key innovations and technologies to watch out for, and share inspiring stories of successful Canadian entrepreneurs who are shaping the future of entrepreneurship in Canada.

20.1 Emerging Trends and Opportunities in the Canadian Market

The Canadian market is ripe with emerging trends and opportunities that present exciting prospects for entrepreneurs. Some of the key trends include:

1. Sustainability and Green Technologies: Increasing consumer demand for sustainable products and services creates opportunities for eco-friendly businesses and green technologies.

2. E-Commerce and Digital Transformation: The continued growth of e-commerce and digital technologies presents opportunities for businesses to reach broader markets and enhance customer experiences.

3. Health and Wellness: With a growing focus on health and wellness, businesses in the health, fitness, and wellness sectors are poised for significant growth.

4. Remote Work and Telecommuting: The rise of remote work has opened up opportunities for businesses that cater to remote workers' needs, such as virtual collaboration tools and coworking spaces.

5. Personalization and Customization: Consumers are seeking personalized experiences, creating opportunities for businesses that offer customizable products or services.

6. Artificial Intelligence and Automation: The integration of AI and automation in various industries presents opportunities for increased efficiency and innovation.

Entrepreneurs who are proactive in embracing these emerging trends can position themselves for success in the Canadian market.

20.2 Innovations and Technologies to Watch Out For

Innovation is the driving force behind entrepreneurship. Some of the technologies and innovations to watch out for in the Canadian entrepreneurial landscape include:

1. Internet of Things (IoT): IoT technology connects devices and systems, enabling businesses to collect and analyze real-time data for better decision-making.

2. Blockchain: Blockchain technology offers secure and transparent transactions, creating new possibilities for industries like finance, supply chain, and healthcare.

3. 5G Technology: The rollout of 5G networks will enable faster and more reliable communication, leading to advancements in various sectors, including healthcare, transportation, and entertainment.

4. Augmented Reality (AR) and Virtual Reality (VR): AR and VR applications have the potential to revolutionize industries like gaming, education, and retail.

5. Clean Energy and Renewable Resources: Advances in clean energy and renewable resources can revolutionize energy production and consumption, offering opportunities for innovative entrepreneurs in the energy sector.

20.3 Inspiring Stories of Successful Canadian Entrepreneurs

Canadian entrepreneurship is rich with inspiring success stories.

Entrepreneurs who have overcome challenges, taken risks, and achieved remarkable success serve as inspirations for aspiring business owners. Some of these stories include:

1. Tobias Lütke - Shopify: Tobias Lütke co-founded Shopify, an e-commerce platform that empowers businesses to create and manage online stores. His vision and dedication have transformed Shopify into a global e-commerce giant.

2. Michele Romanow - Clearbanc: Michele Romanow is the co-founder of Clearbanc, a financial technology company that provides funding to startups and small businesses based on their data.

3. Harley Finkelstein - Shopify: Harley Finkelstein serves as the President of Shopify and has played a crucial role in driving the company's growth and success.

4. Ryan Holmes - Hootsuite: Ryan Holmes founded Hootsuite, a social media management platform used by businesses worldwide, and has been a prominent figure in the social media and tech space.

5. Jean-Christophe Bédos - Birks Group: Jean-Christophe Bédos revitalized the Canadian luxury jewelry brand Birks Group, positioning it as a prominent player in the global luxury market.

These inspiring entrepreneurs demonstrate the limitless potential and boundless creativity of Canadian entrepreneurship, inspiring others to pursue their business dreams and make a positive impact on the world.

In conclusion, the future of Canadian entrepreneurship is bright, filled with emerging trends, innovative technologies, and inspiring entrepreneurs who are reshaping the business landscape. By staying abreast of market opportunities, embracing innovation, and drawing inspiration from successful entrepreneurs, aspiring business owners can carve their path to success and contribute to Canada's dynamic entrepreneurial ecosystem. The journey of entrepreneurship is filled with challenges and opportunities, but with passion, resilience, and a commitment to excellence, Canadian entrepreneurs are well-positioned to create a lasting legacy and shape the future of business in Canada and beyond.

Epilogue: Your Journey as a Canadian Entrepreneur

Congratulations on your journey as a Canadian entrepreneur! As you reach the conclusion of this chapter in your life, take a moment to reflect on your progress, achievements, and the impact you've made on the Canadian business landscape.

Throughout this entrepreneurial journey, you've faced challenges and obstacles, but you've also experienced moments of triumph and success. Celebrate your accomplishments and the growth you've achieved, both as a business leader and as an individual. Your resilience, determination, and willingness to adapt have been essential in navigating the ever-changing business landscape.

In the world of business, continuous learning and growth are the keys to staying competitive and innovative. Embrace a mindset of lifelong learning, always seeking new knowledge, and staying abreast of emerging trends and technologies. Keep an open mind and be willing to explore new opportunities and possibilities. Remember, the business world is dynamic, and embracing change is essential to remain relevant and successful.

As a Canadian entrepreneur, you are not just building a business; you are also contributing to the Canadian economy and society. Your efforts create job opportunities, drive innovation, and stimulate economic growth. By offering valuable products and services, you are positively impacting the lives of your customers and the communities you serve.

As you continue your entrepreneurial journey, remember the importance of corporate social responsibility and sustainability. Make a positive impact on the environment and society by adopting ethical practices, supporting local initiatives, and giving back to the community. Be a role model for responsible business conduct and inspire others to follow suit.

Your journey as a Canadian entrepreneur is more than just

financial success; it is about creating a meaningful and lasting legacy. As you build your business and make an impact, remember to take care of yourself and find balance between your professional and personal life. Remember to prioritize your well-being and make time for your passions and loved ones.

Finally, surround yourself with a supportive network of mentors, advisors, and like-minded entrepreneurs. Connect with fellow business owners, share experiences, and learn from each other's successes and challenges. Collaboration and networking can lead to valuable insights and opportunities for growth.

As you look forward to the future, embrace the excitement of the unknown and the possibilities that lie ahead. The entrepreneurial journey is a remarkable one, filled with opportunities for personal and professional growth. Stay true to your vision, values, and purpose, and let your passion drive you to new heights of success.

Thank you for embarking on this journey as a Canadian entrepreneur. Your courage, dedication, and commitment to excellence make you a true driving force in the Canadian business landscape. Here's to your continued success, growth, and positive impact on the Canadian economy and society. Keep aspiring, keep innovating, and keep making a difference!

Manufactured by Amazon.ca
Bolton, ON

40336174R00042